LAW  E

By

ALVA J. McCLAIN

Founder and First President
Grace Theological Seminary

BMH BOOKS
WINONA LAKE, INDIANA 46590

ISBN: 978-088469-001-6

Contents

Introduction

AMONG CAREFUL STUDENTS of the Scriptures and church history, regardless of their theological bias, there has always been general agreement that if there is any outstanding characteristic term in Christianity, that term is "grace." In much of the New Testament this term becomes almost a synonym for Christianity itself. Thus in some of the Pauline epistles there are benedictions which mention "grace" alone, with the implication that this term covers everything in the Christian faith, and that if we have "grace" nothing else is needed.

As to the meaning of the term as used in the New Testament writings, there is also general agreement. Grace is the unmerited favor of God in Christ. Salvation by grace, therefore, is not of ourselves, not of works, but the gift of God (Eph. 2:8-9). And if Christian salvation is by grace, then it is not of works; "otherwise grace is no more grace" (Rom. 11:6).

Much of the controversy which has attended the Christian doctrine of salvation by grace has arisen about the place of the "law" in relation to the Christian believer who is saved by grace. This was true in the days of the apostles, and it has likewise been true down through the centuries of church history. This was the subject of discussion in the first church council recorded in Acts 15:5, 11. It was also the occasion of the writing of Paul's sharpest epistle, the letter to the Galatian churches. This is an endless battle, but every generation in the church of God must meet the issue for itself.

Various motives—some good and some evil—have raised the issue. Recently it has been raised by teachers and writers with the best of intentions. These men have been grieved and disturbed by the failure of Christian people to live the kind of life the Word of God expects of those saved by grace. As a remedy for this distressing condition in the churches they have proposed that we turn back to the law. We have failed, they argue, because we have not laid upon the members of the churches the *obligations* of the "moral law." The path of success in both the Christian life and the work of the church, they say, will be found in getting the Christian people to see that they are still *under the moral law of God.* It is quite astonishing to find how widely that this opinion is held and advocated.

Although I have always held some very decided opinions in this area of Christian doctrine, the present situation has led me to restudy the entire subject of the law in relation to the Christian believer. The results of this study are presented here with the sincere hope that both the writer and those who read may find the path of truth as revealed in the Word of God.

ALVA J. McCLAIN

CHAPTER 1

"The Law" in New Testament Usage

1. "THE LAW" is the written Mosaic law, including generally the entire Pentateuch. In Galatians 3:10 the writer identifies the law with the entire "book of the law." Our Lord speaks of "the law, or the prophets," identifying the law with that part of our Old Testament comprised in its first five books, a well-known division in His day (Matt. 5:17). The same identification appears in Luke 24:44 and Acts 28:23.

In addition, each one of the five books of the Pentateuch is identified as a portion of "the law." When Paul in I Corinthians 14:34 commands the women "to be under obedience, as also saith the law," he undoubtedly is referring to Genesis 3:16. And quoting from Exodus 20:17 he speaks of it as "the law" (Rom. 7:7). Our Lord Himself refers a lawyer to a passage in Leviticus 19:18, indicating that it was "written in the law" (Luke 10:26-27). Again in Matthew 12:5 Christ cites a reference in Numbers 28:9-10 and asks the Pharisees whether they had not read it "in the law." Finally, in defense of a paid ministry, Paul quotes a passage from Deuteronomy 25:4, declaring that it was written "in the law of Moses" (I Cor. 9:9).

7

This is not a novel view. Archibald McCaig says that in the Gospels "the word 'law' always refers to the Mosaic law," and that at times it means "the whole of the Pentateuch." As to its usage in the Epistles, McCaig writes that "speaking generally, the word with or without the article is used in reference to the law of Moses."[1] And Salmond argues that "the law" (*ho nomos*) of Ephesians 2:15 is to be "taken in its full sense, not the *ceremonial* law only, but the Mosaic Law as a whole, according to the stated use of the phrase."[2]

It is true that occasionally "the law" seems to refer to the entire Old Testament. Compare John 10:34 with Psalm 82:6 and I Corinthians 14:21 with Isaiah 28:11-12. But even in this rare usage it must be remembered that the whole of Old Testament Scripture assumes the existence of the law, calls men back to the law and threatens the penalties of the law for its violations. Thus the idea of an original Mosaic law is probably never wholly absent from such references.

2. This law is one law—an indivisible unity. While it is unquestionably true that at least three elements—moral, ceremonial and civil—appear within this law, it is wrong to divide it into three laws or, as is popularly done, divide it into two laws, moral and ceremonial.

This is clear from the New Testament references.

[1]"Law, in the New Testament," *International Standard Bible Encyclopaedia* (Chicago: Howard-Severance, 1915), III, 1844, 1848.

[2]Stewart D. F. Salmond, "Ephesians," *The Expositor's Greek Testament,* ed. Robertson Nicoll (4th ed.; London: Hodder and Stoughton, 1917), III, 295.

James declares that "whosoever shall keep the whole law, and yet offend in one point, he is guilty of all" (James 2:10). On the "all" of this text, Oesterley writes that the Greek *"panton"* is equivalent to "all the precepts of the *Torah*."[3] The same viewpoint is expressed by the Apostle Paul in Galatians 5:3, "For I testify again to every man that is circumcised, that he is a debtor to do the whole law." And Christ declares that "whosoever therefore shall break one of these least commandments, and shall teach men so, he shall be called the least in the kingdom of heaven" (Matt. 5:19), thus upholding the essential unity of the law. That the "least commandments" referred to by our Lord are those set forth in the Pentateuch, and not merely those of the "moral law" or the few contained in the Sermon on the Mount, is perfectly clear from the context in verses 17 and 18 of Matthew 5, where the identification is unmistakable. He is speaking about the law of Moses.

Some of the ablest commentators concur in this view. Meyer, writing on Matthew 5:17, says, "In *nomos*, however, to think merely of the moral law is erroneous; and the distinction between the ritualistic, civil and moral law is modern."[4] Peake declares, "This distinction between the moral and ceremonial law has no meaning in Paul."[5] The same view is expressed by Godet, "In general, the

---

[3]William O. E. Oesterley, "James," *The Expositor's Greek Testament*, IV, 441.
[4]H. A. W. Meyer, "Matthew," *Commentary on the New Testament* (New York: Funk and Wagnalls, 1884), I, 120.
[5]A. S. Peake, "Colossians," *The Expositor's Greek Testament*, III, 527.

distinction between the ritual and moral elements of the law is foreign to the Jewish conscience, which takes the law as a divine unity."[6] Thus he argues that Paul must have held this view.

In his able article on New Testament law, J. Denny points out an interesting fact in the New Testament use of the term. With one exception, he maintains, a quotation from the Septuagint Version of Jeremiah 31:33 in Hebrews 8:10 and 10:16, the word "law" in the New Testament is always found in the singular. Another commentator claims, "The law of God . . . is the style of Scripture; a classical writer would say 'the laws' of Athens or of Solon."[7] This almost invariable singular form points to the unity of divine law as opposed to merely human laws.

The passage in Romans 2:15 may be cited as a possible exception to the general usage of "law" as referring to the total law of God. Paul speaks here of "the work of the law written in their hearts," that is, the Gentiles. Would not "the law" in this case be limited to its moral element? I do not think so. The very heart of the Old Testament ceremonial law was sacrifice, and the urge to offer sacrifice is universal, found among all peoples.

3. This one law of God includes appropriate penalties as an integral part in order to enforce its demands. The law of God cannot be separated ·

[6]Frederic L. Godet, *Commentary on St. Paul's Epistle to the Romans*, rev. and ed. Talbot W. Chambers (2d.; New York: Funk and Wagnalls, 1892), p. 144.

[7]James Denny, "Law (in New Testament)," *Dictionary of the Bible*, ed. James Hastings (New York: Charles Scribner's Sons, 1911), III, 73.

from its sanctions, as some have assumed. "As many as are of the works of the law are under the curse" (Gal. 3:10). "The law worketh wrath" (Rom. 4:15). The apostle also refers to the law as "the ministration of death," and "the ministration of condemnation" (II Cor. 3:7, 9). And again he designates it as "the law of sin and death" (Rom. 8:2). As Bishop Moule remarks, "It is the divine law . . . by its very holiness the sinner's doom."[8]

That law cannot be divorced from its proper penalties is also the view of the greatest human legal authorities. John Austin defined law as embodying three essential ideas—command, obligation and sanction.[9] Daniel Webster is reported to have said, "A law without a penalty is simply good advice." In the state of Indiana there was an instructive lesson on exactly this point. The legislators passed a law against the use of daylight saving time but attached no penalty for breaking the law. With tongue in cheek the state officials left their public clocks on standard time (to set the proper example) and went to work an hour earlier. The rest of the people set their watches ahead and laughed at the law. Thus law tended to be brought into contempt.

To emasculate the law of God of its divine penalties and still call it "law" is a serious misnomer. It can only confuse the minds of men and finally bring all law, whether human or divine, into contempt or indifference. Moreover, eventually such a procedure tends to empty the cross of Christ of its

[8]"Romans," *The Cambridge Bible* (London: Cambridge Press, 1911).
[9]"Law, in the New Testament," *International Standard Bible Encyclopaedia*, III, 1844.

deepest meaning. The law loses its absolute holiness, sin loses its awful demerit and Calvary loses its moral glory.

4. The Sermon on the Mount is an interpretation, in part, of the same Mosaic law, with special reference to its original inner meaning. This is clear from our Lord's words in Matthew 5:17-19. In verse 19 He declares that "whosoever therefore shall break one of these least commandments, and shall teach men so, he shall be called the least in the kingdom of heaven." These "commandments" are contained in "the law" referred to in verse 17. It is the Mosaic law, and verse 18 asserts that not "one jot or one tittle" of it can pass away. As Alford points out, "These least commandments" refers to "one jot or tittle above."[10]

In this Sermon on the Mount our Lord is not abolishing the Mosaic law and putting in its place another law of His own, as some have superficially suggested. On the contrary, He is reaffirming in the strongest kind of language the unity and inviolability of the Mosaic law. Sometimes it is argued that Christ made certain changes, for instance, in matters such as divorce (vv. 31-32). But, our Lord, as the divine Giver of that law, only abolished certain concessions which had been made earlier because of the hardness of men's hearts (Matt. 19:8), concessions which were not in harmony with the inner meaning of the original divine law. But that law, in the mind of Christ, still stood in its every jot

[10]Henry Alford, *New Testament for English Readers* (2d ed.; New York: Lee, Shepard and Dillingham, 1872), I, 29, v. 29.

and tittle. And to break one of its least commandments is condemned by Him in unmistakable words.

Furthermore, if we examine the Sermon on the Mount carefully, it becomes clear that all three elements of the Mosaic law are present. That the moral element is present needs no special argument, for the greater part of the sermon is devoted to this element. It is not so generally recognized that the ceremonial element of the Mosaic law is also present. Verses 23 and 24 of Matthew 5 speak of "the altar" and also the "gift" brought by the worshiper to the altar. This is the language of sacrifice, made clearer by the American Standard Version, "If therefore thou art offering thy gift at the altar" (v. 23). H. A. W. Meyer translates as follows: "If thou, then, art about to present thy sacrifice . . ."[11] And Alford declares that "the whole language is Jewish, and can only be understood by Jewish rites."[12]

It is also very clear that the Sermon on the Mount contains references to the civil element of the Mosaic law. In Matthew 5:21 our Lord speaks of certain offenders being "in danger of the judgment." The judgment referred to is "that of the local courts of Deuteronomy 16:18," and the phrase "in danger" means "legally liable to."[13] In the next verse our Lord says that certain other offenders would be "in danger of the council." The "council" here is without question the great court of the Sanhedrin. The

[11]Meyer, *op. cit.,* I, 128, v. 23.
[12]Alford, *op. cit.,* I, 31, v. 24.
[13]Charles John Ellicott, *Commentary on the Whole Bible* (Grand Rapids: Zondervan reprint, 1954), VI, 25.

local Jewish courts had the power of capital punishment, but the special penalty of stoning was reserved for the Sanhedrin. We are thus in the realm of Jewish civil jurisprudence as outlined in the Mosaic law. See Numbers 11:16 for the probable origin of the Sanhedrin composed of 70 members. Furthermore, we find in Matthew 5:35 a reference to Jerusalem as the "city of the great King," indicating the central seat of civil authority in the theocratic kingdom, which that city was historically, and will be once again in the future reestablishment of the kingdom according to the Old Testament prophets.

Not only are the three elements of the Mosaic law present in the Sermon on the Mount, but the penalties of that law also appear. Under the Mosaic law religious and civil authority were one. There was no separation of church and state. Therefore we should expect to find both temporal and eternal sanctions among the penalties of the law. Thus in Matthew 5:25-26 we read of the prison and the discharge of the offender when the penalty had been paid to the uttermost farthing. But in verses 22, 29 and 30 we hear the Lord warning offenders of the penalty of "hell fire." See Deuteronomy 32:22 for the basis of this dreadful penalty of the divine wrath as set forth in the Mosaic law.

5. This same Mosaic law was the law under which our Lord was born and to which He rendered the required obedience.

a. Christ was born under the law. Thus we read in Galatians 4:4 that "God sent forth his Son, made of a woman, made under the law." In the Greek construction the phrase "under the law" is exactly the same as in 5:18 where the believer is said to be "not under the law." The child Jesus was circumcised and offered to God formally in the Jewish temple accompanied by the sacrifice of turtledoves —all done "according to the law of Moses" (Luke 2:21-24). And verse 39 declares that "all things according to the law of the Lord" were duly performed. With reference to His earthly ministry to Israel, the Apostle Paul asserts that Jesus Christ "was a minister of the circumcision for the truth of God, to confirm the promises made unto the fathers" (Rom. 15:8).

b. Our Lord obeyed the Mosaic law. He came not to destroy this law but to "fulfil" it (Matt. 5:17). Whatever else may be included in this pregnant statement, it certainly includes obedience. When He went to the Jordan for baptism, He silenced the protests of John the Baptist by saying, "Suffer it to be so now: for thus it becometh us to fulfil all righteousness" (Matt. 3:15). The "righteousness" here is that which is required by the law. The baptism of John was based on the bath "in water" required by the law for those defiled (Num. 19:19). Our Lord's submission to the ritual bath signified not His own need of cleansing but rather His identification with His sinful people. As He reminded John, "It becometh *us*," not Himself alone. After all, His submission to John's baptism is not any more startling than His participation in the Jewish Passover. Both should speak to us of

His identification with His people, certainly not to any taint of uncleanness in Him.

Finally, as He approached the hour of His death, He commanded His disciples to "prepare us the Passover" (Luke 22:8) in accordance with the requirements of strict Mosaic law. Every detail of that coming feast had to be fulfilled. If "sin is the transgression of the law," we also are reminded in the same context that "in him is no sin" (I John 3:4-5).

c. Christ commanded others to obey the Mosaic law. Here the classic reference is Matthew 5:17-19, where He commands obedience to that law down to the "least" of its commandments. This required obedience included, first, submission to the *moral* element as indicated in our Lord's demand of the rich young ruler to "keep the commandments," referring to the second table of the law (Matt. 19:17-19).

That He also required obedience to the *ceremonial* element is clear from His command to the cleansed leper, "Shew thyself to the priest, and offer the gift that Moses commanded" (Matt. 8:4). And in Matthew 26 we have not only an example of our Lord's own submission to the *civil* authorities, but also His command to Peter not to resist them (vv. 47-52). All this was in full harmony with the injunctions of the Mosaic law which demanded respect to be shown to "the ruler of thy people" (Exodus 22:28).

CHAPTER 2

How the Law Could Give
Eternal Life

1. HYPOTHETICALLY, the law could give life if men
kept it. In Leviticus 18:5 it is written: "Ye shall
therefore keep my statutes, and my judgments:
which if a man do, he shall live in them: I am the
LORD." The same idea is repeated in Ezekiel, "And
I gave them my statutes, and shewed them my judgments, which if a man do, he shall even live in
them" (Ezek. 20:11, 13, 21). Unquestionably our
Lord had the same principle in mind when he said
to the rich young ruler who was seeking eternal life
by works, "If thou wilt enter into life, keep the
commandments" (Matt. 19:17*b*). And these "commandments" were all taken from the Mosaic law.
The Apostle Paul summarizes the testimony, "For
Moses describeth the righteousness which is of the
law, That the man which doeth those things shall
live by them" (Rom. 10:5).

2. But this keeping of the law had to be perfect.
In the first place, it had to include the whole law:
"Cursed is everyone that continueth not in all
things which are written in the book of the law to
do them" (Gal. 3:10). This obedience did not dare
to fail at any point, no matter how small, "For

17

whosoever shall keep the whole law, and yet offend in one point, he is guilty of all" (James 2:10) .

Furthermore, this perfection of obedience included the inward attitude as well as the outward act, the thought as well as the deed (Matt. 5:28) . The question has been raised: Did not the law provide for failure to keep it? The answer is: Yes, in a certain sense, through the ritual of animal sacrifice. But here we must be careful to remember two things: First, the smallest failure meant that the law was broken. Second, the blood of animal sacrifices could never take away sins. The sacrifice prescribed by the law did indeed bear witness to a way of salvation, but that way was wholly outside and apart from all law (Rom. 3:21) .

3. Certainly no man (Christ excepted) ever kept the law in the complete sense. "Sin is the transgression of the law" we are told, and in Christ there is "no sin" (I John 3:4-5) . But with reference to all other men it is just as certain that "all have sinned, and come short of the glory of God" (Rom. 3:23) . This is the testimony of all Scripture from Genesis to Revelation.

4. Actually, then, the law can save no sinner. On this point the witness of the Bible is ample and unbroken. "By the deeds of the law there shall no flesh be justified in his sight" (Rom. 3:20) . "By him all that believe are justified from all things, from which ye could not be justified by the law of Moses" (Acts 13:39) . "But that no man is justified by the law in the sight of God, it is evident: for, The just shall live by faith" (Gal. 3:11) .

So crucially important is this truth that the Holy Spirit repeats it no less than three times within the scope of a single verse in Galatians. "A man is not justified by the works of the law . . . not by the works of the law . . . for by the works of the law shall no flesh be justified" (Gal. 2:16). As a matter of fact, Calvary itself should make this clear to all, "for if righteousness come by the law, then Christ is dead in vain" (Gal. 2:21).

CHAPTER 3

Law Unable to Save Men

1. THERE WAS no defect in the law. "The law of the LORD," we are told, "is perfect" (Ps. 19:7). And there is no question here as to the identity of this "law." It is the well-known law of the Old Testament, the law of Moses. Coming to the New Testament, we read that "the law is good" (I Tim. 1:8), and again, "the law is holy, and the commandment holy, and just, and good" (Rom. 7:12). Here we should note a striking fact. The highest estimate of the law was written by the Apostle Paul, the man who was the surest that this law could in no wise give life and salvation to sinners. The weakness was not in the law.

2. The fatal weakness was in man. After declaring that the law is holy, good, and even "spiritual," the apostle shows in Romans why even such a divine law cannot save. "I am carnal," he says, "sold under sin" (Rom. 7:14). The weakness was in man, not in the law. If the law appears to be weak because it cannot save, the explanation is that "it was weak through the flesh" (Rom. 8:3). That is why the Son of God had to come to do "what the law could not do" (Rom. 8:3). The writer of Hebrews seems to suggest that the first "covenant" (of the

law) was faulty. But he guards from any possible misunderstanding by adding that the real "fault" was with "them," that is, the people (Heb. 8:7-8). We must understand that the whole difficulty is in man, not in the law of God.

3. The law's demands could not be relaxed to accommodate the weakness of men. This is the curious idea that some people hold. Grace, to them, is God's tolerance in lowering the absolute demands of the law to the point where sinners can keep it. Such a misconception dishonors both law and grace. If such a scheme had been possible, there would have been no necessity for the Cross. "If there had been a law given which could have given life," argues Paul, "verily righteousness should have been by the law" (Gal. 3:21*b*). This is made crystal clear in Romans: "There is no respect of persons with God. For as many as have sinned without law shall also perish without law: and as many as have sinned in the law shall be judged by the law" (Rom. 2:11-12). The expression "without law" means without a written law such as the Jew had.

But the apostle shows that even though these Gentiles did not have a written law, nevertheless they had a divine law—"the law written in their hearts" (Rom. 2:14-15). And both Gentiles and Jews in the day of judgment will be held completely accountable and responsible for the law which they had, whether written in a book or in the heart and conscience. There is no respect of persons with God. The law stands inviolable as an expression of the immutable holy nature of God. It will not, and cannot, be adjusted to suit the moral weaknesses of sinners. "Righteousness and justice are the foundation of thy throne," we are reminded in Psalm 89:14 ASV.

The very throne of the eternal God rests upon the inviolability of His own law which is the expression of His divine nature. There can be no tampering with that law, not even by God Himself, in the interest of men who have broken the law. If the salvation of the sinner lies in this direction, as some men suppose, there can be no salvation for anyone.

4. It was necessary, therefore, for God to devise a plan for saving sinners without any relaxation of the law. This brings us to the very heart of the gospel, which is the good news of God. Without the slightest relaxation of the law, the Son of God incarnate at Calvary paid man's obligation to broken law to the last farthing. There was no reduction of the debt through some slippery evasion of the righteous demands of divine law. It was paid in full—Jesus paid it all. "Christ hath redeemed us from the curse of the law, being made a curse for us" (Gal. 3:13). "The Lord hath laid on him the iniquity of us all" (Isa. 53:6*b*).

The death of Christ did more than save sinners; it declared the righteousness of God while He was in the very act of saving sinners, so that God "might be just, and the justifier of him which believeth in Jesus" (Rom. 3:26). Read carefully Romans 3:23-26. Not even an infinite God, absolute Sovereign that He is, could play fast and loose with His own law. Therefore, the law was left standing in all the absolute holiness and severity of its demands. But God in Christ met those demands in our stead. Let us leave the matter where God has left it. Only in this way can "we establish the law" (Rom. 3:31).

It was Isaiah, that prophet who perhaps saw most clearly what God would do at Calvary, who said, "It pleased Jehovah, for his righteousness' sake, to magnify the law, and make it honorable" (Isa. 42: 21 ASV). We shall never understand the full glory of the Cross until we see there, not only the love of God for sinners, but also the righteousness and holiness of God in maintaining the inexorable standards of His own law while at the same time saving sinners who were guilty of breaking it. This is the glory of God's grace.

In Romans 8:3 the apostle speaks of "what the law could not do." The last three words of this quotation represent but one Greek word which means literally "powerlessness." The law of God can do nothing to save sinners. It cannot save us from the guilt of sin. It cannot keep us from the dominion of sin. It cannot provide a sufficient motive for obedience to the law. It cannot supply the power necessary to keep its requirements. It cannot recover us when we break the law. May God open our eyes to understand that our "help cometh from the LORD" (Ps. 121:2). Our only hope is in Him.

CHAPTER 4

The Divine Purpose in Giving the Law

IF THE LAW can neither save us nor help to save us, why should we be concerned about it? Why was the law given? The Apostle Paul, who had most to say about law in the New Testament writings, recognized the legitimacy of this question when he asked, "Wherefore then serveth the law?" (Gal. 3:19a). A literal translation would be, "Why then the law?" Paul has fully answered his own question.

1. The law was added because of transgressions (Gal. 3:19). The verb "added" indicates that the law was not primary in God's dealings with sinners. The covenant and promises of God were first. The law was added. And the divine reason is found in man's "transgressions." This general statement will be amplified in other more specific statements. But the heart of the matter is that the giving of the law is related to man's sin. There is a time element in the matter—the law was given because of transgressions until "the seed should come to whom the promise was made." Thus the giving of the law was neither first nor is it final with God in saving sinners or dealing with the problem of sin. It was

"added" and temporary. This indicates a dispensational aspect.

2. The law was enacted for the lawless and ungodly (I Tim. 1:9-10). The idea in this important passage seems to be primarily that of restraint. Viewing the matter from the social standpoint, this is a highly beneficent purpose. The laws of nations are all imperfect reflections of the divine law and are intended to restrain evil and protect society. And in the administration of law and its penalties, the government official is a "minister of God" (Rom. 13:4).

3. Another purpose of law is to give men "the knowledge of sin" (Rom. 3:20). The Greek term is *epignosis*, suggesting not merely knowledge, but a full knowledge of sin. It is true that men totally without any positive law codes are nevertheless conscious in some degree of the fact that they are sinful. And the law was given to increase and heighten this knowledge. Thus, man becomes more fully conscious of his sin and the need of some help which is outside and beyond the law. In this sense alone, law may be said to prepare lost men for the gospel of Christ by making them more conscious of their need. But no preacher should ever be guilty of preaching law to produce conviction without preaching at the same time the good news of salvation in Christ "without the law." It is fine to show men their need of the Bread of Life, but let us beware of sending them away unfed. And the law by itself does not give bread; it only gives a recipe for

making bread, a work which is totally beyond the ability of sinners.

4. Another purpose served by the law is to show the terrible nature of sin (Rom. 7:8-13). In this remarkable passage the Holy Spirit shows us that although the law was something wholly good, nevertheless the sin of man is of such a terrible character that it actually works through the law, so that the good and holy commandment of the law not only fails to eliminate sin but actually stimulates sin! Quoting the commandment, "Thou shalt not covet," the Apostle Paul affirms that the effect of this command was actually to revive sin instead of killing it—"When the commandment came, sin revived," he cries (Rom. 7:9).

This is the damnable thing about human sin; it can take a holy commandment of God and work that which is evil through the commandment. "Sin, taking occasion by the commandment, wrought in me all manner of concupiscence," Paul writes (Rom. 7:8). Who is there among the saved, enlightened by the Spirit of God, that has not found this true in his own experience? The injunctions of law actually stimulate sin instead of putting an end to it. That is why Paul speaks of the law as "the strength of sin" (I Cor. 15:56).

(*Note:* It may seem that there is a contradiction between paragraphs 2 and 4 above. How can the law both restrain sin and also at the same time stimulate sin? The answer is that the law contains two elements and it has two effects. The two elements are the command and the penalty, and the two effects are internal and external. The command inwardly stimulates the attitude of rebellion in men with sinful natures. On the other hand, the penalty externally restrains the outward act of rebellion. Thus the contradiction is only apparent.)

5. Looking at the matter now from a slightly different standpoint, we find that the law was given to reveal how vast is the number of our sins. "Moreover the law entered, that the offence might abound" (Rom. 5:20). The term "offence" here refers not to sin in general, but rather to every individual act of sin committed under the law. Thus the law by multiplying the requirements of God reveals to men the multitude of their offenses. In this sense, the law does not make men worse than they are, but rather shows more clearly how bad they are already. When Paul writes, "The law entered," he employs a Greek verb which "applies to an actor who does not occupy the front of the stage, but who appears there only to play an accessory part."[14] How true! In dealing with sin, it is the grace of God in Christ which occupies the center of the stage in the divine drama of the ages.

6. The law was given to shut every mouth and establish the guilt of all the world. This is an important function of divine law—"that every mouth may be stopped, and all the world may become guilty before God" (Rom. 3:19). The English word "guilty" has unfortunately been weakened in popular usage. To say that a man is guilty of a specific crime means only, in popular thought, that he com-

14Godet, *op. cit.*, p. 227.

mitted the crime. But in the Bible, as well as in the terminology of our courts, to say that a man is "guilty" means not only that he has broken the law but also that he is under an obligation to suffer the penalty for what he has done. The Greek word is *upodikos,* which may be rendered "under judicial sentence." Thus it is the function of divine law, in whatever form it may be revealed, to bring all the world under the judicial sentence of God. And from this judicial sentence there can be no appeal— every mouth is stopped. It is not difficult to get men to admit they have sinned. It is not so easy to get them to admit that they deserve to be punished for their deeds. This is the real meaning of "guilt," and until we acknowledge our guilt God can do nothing for us.

7. The law was given to set a restraining guard upon men until they find true freedom in Christ by faith (Gal. 3:23-24) . "But before faith came, we were kept under the law, shut up unto the faith which should afterwards be revealed" (Gal 3:23) . Both verbs carry the idea of restraint; we were "kept" and "shut up" as if in a prison or under a military guard.

The 24th verse in the King James Version has been the source of considerable misunderstanding. The apostle certainly did not write, "The law was our schoolmaster to bring us unto Christ." The words "to bring us" do not occur in the original text. This whole idea of the law serving as a schoolmaster conducting the sinner to Christ, as Lightfoot has declared, ought to be "abandoned." The *paida-*

gogos (schoolmaster) of ancient times was a slave who exercised restraint over the child until he was made a son. So the law was the "paidagogos" until Christ came and sonship was acquired by faith in Him.

The law does not bring men to Christ, therefore, but rather imposes a necessary restraint upon them until they find true moral freedom by faith in Christ. (For an excellent discussion of this passage, see Denny's article on Law in Hasting's *Dictionary of the Bible*.) This does not mean that the law has no useful function in the work of bringing men to Christ. The law reveals to men their sin and their doom, and in this sense makes the sinner conscious of his need. But this is not the idea taught in Galatians 3:24.

8. The law was given to bear witness prophetically and typically of salvation by grace in Christ (Rom. 3:21). After showing that the whole world is sinful and guilty before God and that by deeds of law no flesh can be justified in His sight, the apostle proceeds to outline the true way of salvation in Romans 3. He writes, "But now the righteousness of God without the law is manifested, being witnessed by the law and the prophets" (Rom. 3:21).

The first thing to notice here is that God's righteousness which saves sinners is "without the law." The Greek preposition is *choris,* meaning "apart from" in the most absolute sense. It is used in Hebrews 4:15 where our Lord is said to have been tempted in all points as we are, yet "without sin." Thus, the salvation of the believer is as absolutely apart from the law as the character of the Son of God is apart from sin. Just as sin had nothing to do with Christ, even so the law has nothing to do with the righteousness we receive through Christ.

But on the other hand, if the law could make absolutely no contribution to our salvation in Christ, nevertheless this same law did function as a witness to that righteousness—"being witnessed by the law and the prophets" (Rom. 3:21). How did the law bear this "witness"? First, the law bore this witness prophetically. The first great prophecy of salvation in a coming Redeemer is found in the book of the law: "And I will put enmity between thee and the woman, and between thy seed and her seed; it shall bruise thy head, and thou shalt bruise his heel" (Gen. 3:15).

Second, the law witnessed to our great salvation in Christ through types. The entire sacrificial system of the Mosaic law pointed forward to the Lamb of God who taketh away the sin of the world. Thus the law spoke clearly and unmistakably of a divine righteousness bestowed by the grace of God on those who simply believe, while at the same time the law could not make the slightest contribution to that righteousness. The correct formula, therefore, is divine righteousness apart from law but witnessed by the law. The law had only the "shadow of good things to come," but "not the very image" of those things (Heb. 10:1). Let us recognize the value of the shadow, but let us beware even of seeming to put one iota of the shadow in the place of the substance.

CHAPTER 5

God's Written Law and Israel

1. AS A WRITTEN LAW, it was given in the form of a covenant to Israel alone. As a preface to the giving of the "Ten Words" on Sinai, the Lord speaks thus through Moses to Israel: "Thus shalt thou say to the house of Jacob, and tell the children of Israel; . . . Now therefore, if ye will obey my voice indeed, and keep my covenant, then ye shall be a peculiar treasure unto me above all people" (Exodus 19:3, 5). Then after the giving of the law at Sinai, we read that Moses "took the book of the covenant, and read in the audience of the people" (Exodus 24:7). As the giving of the law proceeded, the divine Voice enjoined upon Moses the making of a written record, "Write thou these words: for after the tenor of these words I have made a covenant with thee and with Israel" (Exodus 34:27).

After the completion of the written record, the Levites were commanded, "Take this book of the law, and put it in the side of the ark of the covenant of the LORD your God, that it may be there for a witness against thee" (Deut. 31:26). In his article on the Decalogue, Dr. Sampey writes, "It was to

Israel that the Decalogue was primarily addressed, and not to all mankind."[15]

2. This divine covenant set forth in the Pentateuch is clearly described as a legal matter. Thus the Ten Commandments are spoken of as "the tables of the covenant which the Lord made with you" (Deut. 9:9). And the legal record is referred to variously as "the book of the covenant" (Exodus 24:7) and "the words of the covenant" (Deut. 29:1). Furthermore, the penalties of the divine law are called "the curses of the covenant" (Deut. 29:21). Finally, the blood of the animals sacrificed in obedience to the law is characterized as "the blood of the covenant" (Exodus 24:8). And the ark, which stands as a symbol of both moral and ceremonial law, is named "the ark of the covenant" (Num. 10:33).

3. Regarded as a covenant, the blessings of the law were conditional, dependent on Israel's obedience. "If ye will obey my voice indeed, and keep my covenant, then ye shall be a peculiar treasure unto me above all people: . . . a kingdom of priests, and an holy nation" (Exodus 19:5-6). "If thou shalt hearken diligently . . . to observe and to do all his commandments . . . all these blessings shall come on thee" (Deut. 28:1-2). See Deuteronomy 28:1-14. On the other hand, if the people of Israel find themselves groaning under the judgments of God, they must understand that all this is come upon them because "They kept not the covenant of God, and refused to walk in his law" (Ps. 78:10).

[15]John R. Sampey, "The Ten Commandments," *International Standard Bible Encyclopaedia*, V, 2944B.

4. Viewed as a law code, it was given to Israel because of sin. In answering the question, Wherefore then the law? Paul says "It was added because of transgressions" (Gal. 3:19). When the children of Israel left the bondage of Egypt, their deliverance and exodus was accomplished in accordance with the gracious promise of a sovereign God. But how did they react to this undeserved deliverance? The sorry record in Exodus tells of their fearful wish to be back under the bondage of Egypt rather than face the perils of Pharaoh's host, their petulant murmuring against Moses because of the bitter waters at Marah, their lusting after the fleshpots of Egypt, their readiness to stone Moses because of their thirst in the desert—all this in the face of the Lord's mighty working of miracles in delivering them over and over. It was the transgressions of Israel that brought them to the foot of Sinai, for they continually failed to walk by faith under the gracious promises of a sovereign God. Strongly reminiscent of their failure is the warning of Hebrews 12:15, "Looking diligently lest any man fail of the grace of God." No other failure can be so disastrous in the moral and spiritual realm.

5. The giving of this legal covenant to Israel, however, did not abrogate the earlier Abrahamic covenant which was unconditional. In its initial and original form, this covenant with Abraham is found in Genesis 12:1-3. Its sevenfold blessing is not conditioned upon any legal perfection of Abraham. God simply announces what He will do for the patriarch and his seed. It might be argued

that there is, after all, one condition laid down in verse 1, "Get thee out of thy country, and from thy kindred . . . unto a land that I will shew thee." But Abraham's compliance with this injunction was only his response of faith to the sovereign promises of God. "By faith Abraham . . . went out, not knowing whither he went" (Heb. 11:8). (In the same way we respond by faith today to the call of God when we leave the world and enter that blessed realm designated "in Christ.") Now this covenant with Abraham was made 430 years before the law was given at Sinai, and Paul argues that this "law . . . cannot disannul [the covenant], that it should make the promise of none effect" (Gal. 3:17). Even the Mosaic law itself witnesses to the supremacy of the former covenant. In spite of Israel's iniquities and the certainty of divine judgment upon the nation, the Lord declares, "My covenant with Abraham will I remember; . . . yet for all that, when they be in the land of their enemies, I will not cast them away, neither will I abhor them, to destroy them utterly, and to break my covenant with them: for I am the LORD their God" (Lev. 26:42, 44).

6. The Israelite is "under" this Mosaic written law until he finds forgiveness and freedom in the "new covenant" under grace in Christ. "Know ye not, brethren, (for I speak to them that know the law,) how that the law hath dominion over a man as long as he liveth?" (Rom. 7:1). Freedom from the law's bondage comes only as the Jew becomes "dead to the law by the body of Christ" (Rom.

7:4). The same general idea is asserted in Galatians 5:3, "For I testify again to every man that is circumcised, that he is a debtor to do the whole law." The reference is not merely to the physical operation, but to submission to the rite with the belief that it will either save or help to save the soul. Such a one is bound by the entire law, to do it all or suffer the penalty for failure.

It is clear that Paul regarded the unsaved Jews of his day as being under the law, for he says in Romans 3:19, "We know that what things soever the law saith, it saith to them who are under the law." The Greek verbs here indicate a present reality, not merely a relationship which once existed but is no longer in force.

At the very moment the apostle was writing, the law was speaking to his unsaved kinsmen who, he argues, "are under the law." If this were not so, there could be no day of judgment for them, as he affirms there certainly shall be: "As many as have sinned under the law shall be judged by the law" (Rom. 2:12*b* ASV). The same thought appears in Galatians 4 where Paul, speaking of the "Jerusalem which now is," says she "is in bondage with her children" (Gal. 4:25). That this is the bondage of the law is clear from the context, especially in Galatians 5:1, where he warns the saved not to go back to it.

This view does not conflict in any way with the fact that what we call the Dispensation of Law ended at Calvary. For God may change in his way of dealing with men without totally abolishing the main feature of a former dispensation. Conscience was not abolished when human government was established. Nor were the promises abrogated when the Dispensation of Law began. So today, in this Age of Grace, there is still law for those who will not come to Christ for freedom. And if when men believe, they are "made dead to the law" (Rom. 7:4 ASV) in order that they may be joined to Christ, then this dominion of the law must be a very genuine and present reality.

CHAPTER 6

The Mosaic Law and Gentiles

THE RELATION of the Mosaic law to Gentiles is important and there has been some sharp disagreement on the subject. Some assert that not only was the written Mosaic law given to Israel alone, but that it also has no relation whatsoever to Gentiles. Others argue that this law is for all men and is universal in its obligations. There is some truth on both sides.

1. The law of Moses, in a certain sense, made provision for Gentiles to enter into its benefits and restraints. This provision, under the historical theocratic kingdom, is a well-attested fact. Thus, in the law concerning the Passover, provision was made for "the stranger" who might sojourn with Israel; and there was to be one law for "homeborn" and "stranger" (Exodus 12:48-49). Also, in the case of freewill offerings unto the Lord for burnt offerings, the laws concerning perfect and imperfect animals applied to both Israel and the strangers in Israel alike (Lev. 22:18-22). Regulations dealing with the blood from animal sacrifices were imposed upon the stranger—"Whatsoever man there be of the house of Israel, or of the strangers which sojourn among you, that offereth a burnt-offering or sacrifice, . . . that eateth any manner of blood; I will even set my face against that soul that eateth blood, and will

cut him off from among his people" (Lev. 17:8, 10).
Quite evidently the "stranger," under some circum-
stances, must have been permitted to join in the
sacrificial rites.

Furthermore, from Deuteronomy 23:1-7 it appears that certain restrictions surrounded the reception of outsiders "into the congregation of the
LORD," showing that such a reception was possible.
The Prophet Isaiah seems to level whatever distinction there remained between the Israelite and the
"son of the stranger, that hath joined himself to
the LORD" (Isa. 56:3). The latter is not to say,
"The LORD hath utterly separated me from his people" (Isa. 56:3). The chief point under consideration in the passage is the keeping of the legal sab-
bath (Isa. 56:2).

With these many clear provisions for "the stranger" written in the Jewish Scriptures, it is difficult
to understand how such a violent antagonism
against Gentiles could develop as appeared in the
days of Christ.

(*Note:* Some interpreters have regarded the law
as something which raised an insuperable barrier
between Jew and Gentile on the basis of Ephesians
2:11-19. The misleading translation of verse 14 in
the King James Version has doubtless contributed
to this wrong idea. "For he [Christ] . . . hath made
both one, and hath broken down the middle wall
of partition between us; having abolished in his
flesh the enmity, even the law of commandments
contained in ordinances" (Eph. 2:14-15). The
"middle wall of partition" is not "between us," that

is, between Jew and Gentile, as the words suggest. This "middle wall" is certainly "the law of commandments" mentioned in verse 15, which was "abolished" by the death of Christ. But this "middle wall" of "law" did not merely separate one kind of sinners (Jews) from another kind of sinners (Gentiles). It was rather a barrier which separated all sinners, both Jew and Gentile, from a holy God. That is why the "law of commandments" had to be abolished in order to "reconcile both [Jew and Gentile] unto God in one body" (Eph. 2:16).

2. But even entirely apart from any provision made by the law for "strangers" to sojourn with Israel, the great underlying principles of the Mosaic written law were found reflected in some degree in Gentile morality and religion. The Mosaic law had three elements: the moral, ceremonial and civil. Discussing the case of the Gentiles, Paul declares that sometimes "the Gentiles, which have not the law [that is, the written law], do by nature the things contained in the law" (Rom. 2:14). In so acting, Paul argues, the Gentiles "shew the work of the law written in their hearts" (Rom. 2:15). Thus, Paul claims everything good that has ever appeared in the Gentile world as a reflection, however faint, of the one original divine law recorded in Scripture. Now it is a fact that among the pagan Gentile nations there is found occasionally a fairly high knowledge of morality—a reflection of the moral element which appears perfectly in the law written in Scripture. Also the urge to offer sacrifice is universal, found among all nations—a reflection of the cere-

monial law in Scripture. Finally, in the civil codes of various nations reflections may be seen of the written law of God (cf. the remarkable code of Hammurabi). All this points back to the unity of the divine law, both in its content and its original source. In the one case it is written perfectly in Scripture. In the other it is written imperfectly in the hearts of men. There is one divine law, not two.

3. Therefore, we must conclude that even the Gentiles were and are "under law," but in a somewhat different sense from the Jews. At this point one should carefully study the material in Romans 2:11-15. Here both Jews and Gentiles are being considered as sinners apart from Christ. The Jews had the perfect divine law written in Scripture, and by that law they will be judged (v. 12*b*). The Gentiles did not have such a law, but they will perish for their sins nevertheless (v. 12*a*). Answering the objection that this does not seem fair to the Gentiles, Paul says that although they were without the written law of Scripture, they nonetheless had a law—the law written in their hearts, an inner law which reflected imperfectly the written law of God. And by this law they will be judged and condemned, because they violated the inner law of which the conscience within them bore witness (vv. 14-16). Thus there is no respect of persons with God. Judged by the light they had (one in its original source), all men must perish, whether Jew or Gentile. The only hope for sinners is not in the law, but in the grace of God in our Lord Jesus Christ.

CHAPTER 7

The Christian and the Law

1. SEVERAL ANSWERS, all evasive in character, have been given to the question: Is the Christian believer under the law? For the most part they are based upon wrong or inadequate definitions of law.

a. Some argue that the believer is under the moral law, but not under the ceremonial law.

b. Others say that we are under the moral *law,* but not under its penalties.

c. Still others assert that we are under the moral law as a rule of life, but not as a way of salvation. Another way of saying the same thing is that we are under the law for sanctification but not for justification.

d. Another view is that we are under the Sermon on the Mount, but not under the law of Sinai.

e. A rather curious view advanced recently is that the Christian believer is under "the law of God," but not under the "law of Moses." According to this scheme the "law of Moses" is the entire system of law recorded in the Pentateuch, whereas the "law of God" is limited to the Ten Commandments![16] That such a distinction between the "law

[16]See Arthur W. Pink, *The Law and the Saint* (Swengel, Pa.: Reiner Publications, n.d.)

of God" and the "law of Moses" cannot stand is clear from the Scriptures. See Luke 2:21-24, 39 where the same law is called variously the "law of Moses" and the "law of the Lord," and the law under consideration is ceremonial in nature. See also Mark 7:8-13 where what "Moses said" is also identified as the "commandment of God," and the material quoted from the Pentateuch includes one of the Ten Commandments and also a death penalty from the civil code. We will not be misled by any of the above erroneous views if we hold fast to a complete definition of the divine law, namely, that the law of God in the Bible is one law, including moral, ceremonial and civil elements, and inseparable from its penalties.

2. The meaning of the Biblical phrase "under the law." This expression occurs twelve times in the King James Version, fourteen times in the American Standard Version. Twice the Greek preposition is *en* (Rom. 2:12 ASV; 3:19), eleven times it is *hupo* with the accusative case (Rom. 6:14-15; I Cor. 9:20 ASV; Gal. 3:23, 4:4-5, 21, 5:18). In the remaining passage the English phrase "under the law" represents a very dubious translation of a single Greek word (I Cor. 9:21), which will be discussed later.

According to Green, the *en* of the above texts refers to the *sphere* in which the subject is dwelling and acting.[17] This would accurately describe the Jew in relation to the divine law. He was not only

[17]S. G. Green, *Handbook to the Grammar of the Greek Testament* (New York: Fleming H. Revell, rev. 1912), p. 240.

under the law, but also *in* the law as the sphere of his existence and actions.

The preposition *hupo* with the accusative in the other texts means *"subject* to the power of any person or thing." Thayer cites as examples the very references under consideration in this study.[18] An excellent illustration may be found in Matthew 8:9, where the Roman centurion says, "For I am a man under [*hupo*] authority, having soldiers under [*hupo*] me." Just as the centurion was absolutely under Roman military authority, both as to its laws and its penalties, so also were his soldiers under his authority.

In summary we may say that for one to be "under the law" in the Biblical sense is to be under the law of God—the entire Mosaic legal system in its indivisible totality—subject to its commands and liable to its penalties.

3. Now the Word of God declares plainly that the Christian believer is not "under the law." At least four times, simply and without qualification, the New Testament asserts this great truth: "For ye are not under the law" (Rom. 6:14). "Because we are not under the law" (6:15). "Ye are not under the law" (Gal. 5:18). "Not being myself under the law" (I Cor. 9:20 ASV). *(Note:* This last statement is not in the King James Version. But practically all the great editors of the Greek text of the New Testament agree that the clause was a part of the original sacred text. It was probably omitted from

[18]J. H. Thayer, *Greek-English Lexicon of the New Testament* (New York: Harper & Bros., 1889), p. 642.

a few of the Greek manuscripts by legalistically-inclined scribes. The American Standard Version includes it in I Corinthians 9:20 without either an alternative reading or other marginal note, thus indicating the translators' unquestioned judgment that it belongs there as a part of the inerrant Word of God through the Apostle Paul.) It should also be noted that in two of the above quoted texts, the writer ties two great facts of the Christian faith directly to the truth that "we are not under the law." In Romans 6:14 the Christian's deliverance from the lordship of sin is tied to his deliverance from the law, and in Galatians 5:18 our deliverance from the law is regarded as an evidence of our being led by the Spirit. These practical effects in the realm of the moral and spiritual life will be discussed more fully.

a. Consider further that the Christian believer is not under law in any sense as a means of salvation or any part of it. In Romans 3:20 we read that "by the deeds of the law . . . shall no flesh be justified in his sight." And in this text the Holy Spirit seems to broaden sweepingly the exclusion of all deeds of all law from the divine act in the justification of sinners. There are no definite articles. The Greek text reads simply "by deeds of law." Again in Romans 6:14 the Scripture declares not only that the law as law has absolutely nothing to contribute in the accomplishment of the believer's sanctification, but on the contrary that freedom from the law's bondage is actually one indispensable factor in that important work of God in the soul. Still further, when Paul comes to deal with the matter of Christian security in Romans 8, he asserts that the law has no power to keep us in safety, but "what the law could not do" in this regard, God sent His Son to accomplish for us and also in us (Rom. 8:3-4). Thus we see that the law can neither justify, sanctify nor preserve us.

b. The law can give no help to men as a means of salvation from sin. In Colossians 2:14 who can fail to see the reference to Sinai in the phrase "handwriting of ordinances"? The apostle declares that this same divine law was not only "against us" but also "contrary to us." And the same writer, referring to the Decalogue "written and engraven in stones," describes it as a "ministration of death" (II Cor. 3:7). In Romans 4:15 we learn that the law "worketh wrath," and in Galatians 3:12 that "the law is not of faith." And when certain men arose in the early church to insist that believers should be placed under at least a small part of the law, Peter himself rebuked them with the reminder that this law was "a yoke . . . which neither our fathers nor we were able to bear" (Acts 15:10).

c. According to the New Testament, the Christian is "delivered from the law." This is the central argument of Romans 7. Any failure to see and accept it leads inevitably to that moral and spiritual defeat pictured so vividly later in the chapter. Those believers had not learned that "ye also are become dead to the law by the body of Christ" (v. 4), and that "we are delivered from the law" (v. 6). Both verbs are in the aorist tense, pointing back to something done once for all. The same book sums up the argument in one irrefutable statement, "Christ is the end of the law for righteousness to everyone that believeth" (Rom. 10:4). The Greek arrangement of the words here puts the word "end" first in the sentence. That is where the emphasis must be put—the end of the law has come for all believers in Christ. God says "end." Let there be no equivocation here. Either this is true or there is no salvation for sinners.

d. The conclusion must be that the law itself as law, for the Christian, has been "abolished." No one can read II Corinthians 3 with an unprejudiced attitude and not see that the writer is discussing the very center of the law of God with its "tables of stone" (v. 3). All this, so far as the Christian believer is concerned, has been "done away" (v. 11); it has been "abolished" (v. 13). The same thing is set forth in Ephesians 2:15, "Having abolished in his flesh the enmity, even the law of commandments contained in ordinances." And again we read that "the handwriting of ordinances that was against us" has been blotted out, nailed to the cross of Christ (Col. 2:14). In so doing, our blessed Lord spoiled the powers of darkness and triumphed over them. For the great accuser of the brethren and his hosts had found his base of operations in the law. Under the law he could rightly argue that we sinners deserved to be judged and forever doomed. But, thank God, all this is ended for the believer. Every penalty of the divine law has been paid, every demand of the law has been satisfied—not **by** us, but by the Lamb of God.

(*Note:* It has been argued by some that the above quoted texts refer only to the ceremonial element of the law and not the moral law. Here again I refer the reader back to my earlier argument for the unity of the divine law. Also, on Colossians 2:14, Peake says, "This distinction between the moral and ceremonial law has no meaning in Paul. The Law is a unity and is done away as a whole." On the clause "took it out of the way," he comments, "The change from aorist to perfect [tense] is significant as expressing the abiding character of the abolition." For the Christian there can be no "point of return" back to the law as law. On the clause "nailing it to his cross," Peake adds, "When Christ was crucified, God nailed the Law to His cross. Thus it, like the flesh, was abrogated, sharing His death. The bond therefore no longer exists for us."[19])

4. In what sense were God's people "under the law" in the Old Testament age? This is a question which will inevitably be raised at this point. And it is a legitimate question which should be answered.

a. Let us note that God had a people in Old Testament days and that this people was "under the law" from Sinai to Calvary. This is the substance of Paul's argument in Galatians 3:17-23. Speaking of that Old Testament people, with whom he himself had been once associated, Paul writes,

[19]Peake, *op. cit.*, p. 527-28.

"But before [the] faith came, we were kept under the law" (v. 23).

b. Consider now that in these Old Testament days the phrase "under the law" could have had only two possible meanings—either "under the law" as a way of salvation, or "under the law" as a rule of life.

c. We can be certain that "under the law" in those days could not have meant a way of salvation. For nothing is taught more clearly in the Word of God than that no one in any age could be saved by law-keeping. "By the deeds of the law there shall no flesh be justified in his sight" (Rom. 3:20). The entire fourth chapter of Romans is given to the proposition that both Abraham and David were saved by faith, not by law. With this possibility excluded, there is only this possible alternative: "Under the law" for these Old Testament people meant that they were under it as a *rule of life.*

d. Let us follow now the argument to its logical conclusion. The dispensational change from the Age of the Law to the Age of Grace does *not* mean that formerly sinners were saved by deeds of law whereas today they are saved by grace, for we have already seen that men could not be saved by law in any age! But it does mean that God's people in the former age were "under the law" as a rule of life, whereas today they are not "under the law" as a rule of life. Yet this is the very sense in which the legalistic theology of our day affirms that the law is still in force over the Christian believer!

What utter nonsense! If their affirmation be true,

then the distinction between being "under law" and not being "under law" has been canceled, and the Apostle Paul wasted his time writing the great books of Romans and Galatians, to say nothing of the other books which declare the vital importance of this distinction.

CHAPTER 8

Dangers of Putting Christians Under the Law

1. THERE ARE AT LEAST three possible ways in which a theological system can be constructed for the purpose of putting the Christian under law:

a. A system which would place the Christian under the total law, including all its elements and penalties. This is pure Judaism.

b. A system which would place the Christian under the moral law and its penalties. This is moral legalism.

c. A system which would place the Christian under the moral law stripped of its proper penalties. This might be called a "weak and beggarly" legalism (cf. Gal. 4:9).

2. It is this third system that deserves the severest criticism.

a. It employs an un-Scriptural terminology, taking only one element of the law and divesting even that of its sanctions, and then calls it "the law of God." In the Bible "the law" is a unity which includes all its elements with its penalties.

b. Claiming to honor the law of God, the system actually dishonors the law, especially because it reduces the holy law of a holy God to the level of mere good advice, comparable to some of the legalistic functions of the United Nations organization.

c. This ultimately moves in the direction of theological disaster, bringing and compounding confusion into our views of sin, of salvation, of the work of Christ and even of the doctrine of God.

d. Worst of all, this abstraction of the moral element from the ceremonial element in Old Testament law, and its imposition upon the Christian as a rule of life, has a grave spiritual and moral danger. For it is precisely this ceremonial element which provides the context of grace for the moral element, and this context of grace provides the great motivating principle which secures the fulfillment of the moral element of the law. Thus this kind of legalistic morality defeats itself.

3. The Word of God condemns unsparingly all attempts to put the Christian believer "under the law." The Holy Spirit through the Apostle Paul gave to the church the book of Galatians for the very purpose of dealing with this heresy. Read this epistle over and over, noting carefully the precise error with which the writer deals. It is not a total rejection of the gospel of God's grace and a turning back to a total legalism. It is rather the error of saying that the Christian life, having begun by simple faith in Christ, must thereafter continue under the law or some part of it. This is clear from the apostle's indignant charge: "This only would I learn of you, Received ye the Spirit by the works

of the law, or by the hearing of faith? Are ye so foolish? having begun in the Spirit, are ye now made perfect in the flesh?" (3:2-3). Little wonder that he begins the chapter with a cry of astonishment, "O foolish Galatians, who hath bewitched you, that ye should not obey the truth . . .?" (3:1).

And having pursued his devastating argument against this type of legalism through chapter 3 and into chapter 4, showing that the redemption of God in Christ has set us free from all the bondage of the law, he again asks with irony, "But now, after that ye have known God, or rather are known of God, how turn ye again to the weak and beggarly elements, whereunto ye desire again to be in bondage?" (4:9). And then he adds, "I am afraid of you, lest I have bestowed upon you labour in vain" (4:11). "Ye did run well; who did hinder you that ye should not obey the truth?" (5:7). As for the preacher who had introduced this heresy among the flock, Paul writes by inspiration of the Holy Ghost, "He that troubleth you shall bear his judgment, whosoever he be" (5:10).

That this matter was no mere case of theological hairsplitting (as some today are accustomed to charge) is made clear in the very beginning of the book of Galatians. In seeking to add some modicum of law to the gospel of God's grace, these legalistic teachers are preaching "another gospel" (1:6). Paul hastens, however, to add that what they are preaching is really "not another" gospel at all, for the very meaning of the term "gospel" excludes all works of law. And so, strange as it may seem to some, for anyone to add any law (no matter how worthy) to the simple good news of God's grace in Christ, is actually to destroy the gospel as gospel! It is no longer gospel at all! If even the smallest item of the law should be added to the gospel and made binding upon believers, so that the require-ment now becomes "believe" plus something else in order to be saved, the soul which accepts this "plus something else" automatically becomes "a debtor to do the whole law" (5:3). For such a one, the apostle warns, "Christ shall profit you nothing" (5:2).

And so the problem becomes very simple: Either Christ will save you by grace through faith plus nothing, or He will not save you at all! As a matter of fact, even an omnipotent God can save sinners in only one way—that is, by grace. Because of what God is and because of what we are, there is no other way. Paradoxical as it may seem, this is one place where the addition of something finite actual-ly results in a subtraction which is infinite. Such is the mathematics of grace. If the sinner adds any-thing, he loses everything. If he adds nothing, he wins everything.

Understanding this, we can then accept sympa-thetically the ultimatum of Galatians: "But though we, or an angel from heaven, preach any other gospel unto you than that which we have preached unto you, let him be accursed" (Gal. 1:8).

CHAPTER 9

The Standard of Life for Christians

THIS STANDARD is the will of God in the context of His grace given in our Lord Jesus Christ as revealed perfectly in the entire written Word of God. This is so important that it should be memorized. The essential elements are:

a. The will of God.
b. In the context of His grace.
c. Given in our Lord Jesus Christ.
d. Revealed in the entire Word of God written.

Three passages should be read and studied in this connection. The first is Romans 12:1-2, where Paul sets before us as Christian believers what he calls "the will of God." But it should be noticed that this "will" of God is enshrined within "the mercies of God." The "mercies" are first. For saved sinners this is the order of approach to the "will of God." The first eleven chapters of Romans are devoted to the exposition of the "mercies" of divine grace. Then the apostle takes up the matter of God's will for Christians, and he sets it before us in the very center of the "mercies." In exhorting us to realize the "will of God," he writes, "I beseech you . . . by the mercies of God." This is what we mean by "the will of God in the context of His grace."

The second passage is John 5:39 (ASV), where our Lord declares Himself as the central object and theme of all written revelation. To the Jewish hearers of His day, men who prided themselves on their zeal in study of the written Word, He says, "Ye search the scriptures, because ye think that in them ye have eternal life." And then He reminds them that these same Scriptures "are they which bear witness of me." If they miss Him, all their zealous searching of Scripture will count for nothing. For the gift of eternal life comes only by divine grace, and the grace of God comes only in His Son our Lord Jesus Christ. Thus the will of God in the context of His grace is found in Christ alone. "Grace . . . came by Jesus Christ" (John 1:17).

The third passage is II Timothy 3:16-17, where the Holy Ghost through Paul affirms that "All scripture is given by inspiration of God, and is profitable" in every way for the children of God, to bring them to perfection and furnish them unto all good works.

Consider now these important truths found in the above three passages:

1. The entire written Word of God is able to make us "wise" with reference to that salvation which we have by faith in Christ. It is undoubtedly true that a sincere perusal of the Scriptures can, under the guidance of the Holy Spirit, bring the unsaved to faith in the Lord Jesus Christ. But it is also true that one may in simple faith receive eternal life in Christ and yet remain unwise in many respects with reference to that great salvation. For

this reason God has given us His total written Word to make us "wise" regarding the greatness of our salvation in Christ.

2. This entire Word of God is "profitable" to all Christians in all its various parts. We should notice the sweeping character of the apostle's statement: *"All* scripture . . . is profitable." Or as it is also properly translated, *"Every* scripture . . . is . . . profitable" (ASV). Let us beware, therefore, of the error of supposing that there is anything in the Book of God which can be set aside, or even neglected, by the Christian believer. All of the Book— every part of it, no matter how small—will be found "profitable" for the saved. We cannot dispense with any of it without loss to ourselves. In this connection, it needs to be emphasized without any compromise, that "all scripture" includes the law of Moses. Not only so, but it includes all the elements of that law—moral, ceremonial and civil. And included also are the penalties of the law. We who are saved are not under the law, but the law is part of the written Word and is therefore "profitable" to the saved. In what way is "all scripture" profitable? The answer is: (*a*) "for doctrine," (*b*) "for reproof," (*c*) "for correction," (*d*) "for instruction in righteousness." We find in I Corinthians 10:1-14 an instructive lesson in how Paul used the law of Moses in the Pentateuch in the various ways outlined above for the good of Christian believers in his day. We are not *under* the law; but because that law is inspired Scripture, it is full of valuable doctrine and useful lessons for us.

3. This entire written Word serves as a "mirror" for the Christian. In this perfect mirror of the Scriptures we may see ourselves. Speaking of the Word of God in relation to Christian believers, James describes the man who "beholding his natural face in a glass: . . . and goeth his way and straightway forgetteth what manner of man he was" (James 1:23-24). He contrasts him to the man who not only "looketh" at himself in the mirror but also is a "doer" of something about the matter (1:25). In the beginning, the difference between the two men is not merely a matter of doing or not doing, but rather in the manner in which they look into the mirror of the Word. The Greek verb of verse 24 suggests a merely casual look, whereas the verb of verse 25 indicates a careful look. It is the careful look and continuance therein that produces the "doer of the work" and the resultant blessing.

But this looking at ourselves in the mirror of the Word must not be separated from the look into the same mirror to behold the image of our Lord. Looking at ourselves is not enough and by itself can only bring utter despair. We must see the Lord. And the Holy Scriptures in their totality comprise the perfect mirror in which we may see our Lord in all His grace and glory. As the Apostle Paul writes, "But we all, with open [unveiled] face beholding as in a glass [mirror] the glory of the Lord, are changed into the same image from glory to glory, even as by the Spirit of the Lord" (II Cor. 3:18). Seeing ourselves in the mirror of the Word is very worthwhile, but it is beholding the Lord in this mirror that brings about the moral and spiritual change that all of us need so much. And it is significant that Paul in writing about the importance of this mirror of the Word, has in mind primarily the Old Testament Scriptures, and especially the five books of the Pentateuch written by Moses (cf. vv. 14 and 15).

This brings us to the remarkable character of the truth taught in II Corinthians 3. In the first thirteen verses the apostle declares emphatically that for the Christian believer the law of Moses has been "done away" and actually "abolished" (vv. 11, 13). Yet this same law remains as part of the mirror of the written Word in which we see the glory of the Lord. As "law" it has been abolished; as believers we are no longer under it as "law." Yet it remains as a part of Scripture, and as such it is "profitable" for us because it bears witness to our Lord and Saviour. Thus, to emasculate the written Word or any portion of it, whether moral or ceremonial law or anything else, is to mar and deface to the same extent the only divinely authorized portrait of the Lord Jesus Christ, and in the end to hinder the Spirit's perfect work of sanctification. We see the importance of this in the post-resurrection ministry of our Lord. "Beginning at Moses and all the prophets, he expounded unto them in all the scriptures the things concerning himself" (Luke 24:27). (See also Luke 24:44.)

4. This entire written Word of God points us to a perfect example in Christ. As we behold His glory in the mirror of the Word, we see:

a. What we as believers ought to be here and now. We shall remember that we ought "so to walk, even as he walked" (I John 2:6). We shall not forget that "even hereunto were ye called: because Christ also suffered for us, leaving us an example, that ye should follow his steps" (I Peter 2:21). If we ever expect to have the "mind" in us "which was also in Christ Jesus" (Phil. 2:5), we must find that "mind" in the record of what He was and what He did. And for this we must have more than the four gospels or even the New Testament writings, but the total written Word of God from Genesis through Revelation.

Furthermore, as we see Christ in this total Word we learn:

b. What we shall be at His coming. We shall understand that, against all present appearances and adverse conditions, "when he shall appear, we shall be like him" (I John 3:2). And with this blessed hope in our hearts, we shall become purer men and women here and now even before He comes (I John 3:4). Thus we shall count the "sufferings of this present time" not even "to be compared with the glory which shall be revealed in us" (Rom. 8:18). If God has predestinated us to be "conformed to the image of his Son" (Rom. 8:29), He has also predestinated the *means* by which this blessed conformation is being carried forward even here and now. It is the total Word of God written and inspired, bearing witness of His Son.

5. This total "Word of God written" is given us to center our attention upon Christ, what He is,

what He has done, and what He said. For the true believer, Christ must be the center and circumference of all things. "Thou, O Christ, art all I want; more than all in Thee I find."

a. The written Word fixes our attention on Christ Himself. There are other great figures in the Scriptures. Think of Moses and Elijah, probably the greatest in the halls of Old Testament fame. But even these fade from sight in the light of the glory of the eternal Son. If we read the will of God rightly, led of the Spirit, we shall see "no man, save Jesus only" (Matt. 17:8). Let all those who preach and teach the Word take solemn heed. If they speak of Moses and Elijah and the others, let them be careful so to speak that these "lesser lights" will direct the eyes of men to Him who is both their Lord and ours.

b. The written Word fixes our attention on the love of Christ. Even a lost world recognizes the value of love and its leaders talk much about love. But most of this talk concerns itself with love in the abstract. Sometimes it becomes a mere verbal idolatry. But in the Bible we meet something altogether different. Here we are told indeed that "God is love" (I John 4:8), but we are not left to speculate as to the real nature of "love" in the unseen and ineffable deity. The same Word which tells us that "God is love" goes on to direct our eyes to something historically concrete: "In this was manifested the love of God toward us, because that God sent His only begotten Son into the world, that we might live through him" (I John 4:9). Do we struggle intellectually to understand the real nature of divine love? Well, "herein is love, not that we loved God, but that he loved us, and sent his Son to be the propitiation for our sins" (I John 4:10). And as we behold the love of God incarnate in the Son, our ears become more attentive to the exhortation which follows: "Beloved, if God so loved us, we ought also to love one another" (I John 4:11).

c. The written Word of God also directs our eyes to the work of Christ. No matter where we open the Book, if we have eyes to see, we meet the blood of atonement. John the Baptist, last in the great succession of prophets of the Old Testament, sums up the testimony as his eyes look upon the incarnate Son. "Behold the Lamb of God," John cries, "which taketh away the sin of the world" (John 1:29). And these words upon the lips of John spoke of death, for a "lamb" cannot take away sin except by dying.

Thus, throughout the written Word, wherever we open its pages, "we see Jesus, who was made a little lower than the angels for the suffering of death, crowned with glory and honour; that he by the grace of God should taste death for every man" (Heb. 2:9). And perceiving in Calvary "the love of God, because he laid down his life for us," we are brought to see that "we ought to lay down our lives for the brethren" (I John 3:16).

d. The written Word of God also opens our eyes to the words and commandments of Christ. Our Lord says, "He that hath my commandments, and keepeth them, he it is that loveth me" (John 14:

21) , and again He says, "If a man love me, he will keep my words" (v. 23) . Here again we must have the total Word of God in order to hear in its widest aspect the voice of our Lord. We must understand that the voice of the infinite God comes to men always through the Son, the eternal *logos*.

It is wrong, therefore, to reject the Old Testament or any part of it, as some do, or to set aside the epistles of the New Testament as somehow inferior to the four gospels, or to treat the prophetic element in Scripture as of little or no importance to the Christian life, as others do. As we read the written Word, if we are wise we shall hear the voice of the preexistent Son speaking to us in the Old Testament, the voice of the incarnate Son speaking to us in the gospel records in the days of His flesh, and the voice of the exalted and glorified Son speaking to us from heaven in the other New Testament books.

To be sure, there is progress in the revelation of God through the Son. In the movement of history, some things are superseded; others may be abolished. Some things are more important than other things. We must read the Book of God, not mechanically, but under the guidance of His Holy Spirit.

Sometimes we are asked: "What does it mean to 'keep' the words and commandments of the Lord Jesus Christ?" We can answer that at least one thing it cannot mean is to put ourselves back under any legalistic system of any kind. But positively we have some texts which shed light upon the problem. One is I Kings 14:8, where the Lord speaks of King David as one who "kept my commandments, and who followed me with all his heart, to do that only which was right in mine eyes." This is God's pronouncement upon the total life of David, a man who had failed terribly more than once.

Another passage is found in the New Testament in John 17:6. Here we stand upon solemn ground and hear the communings of deity, the Son reporting and praying to the Father. And concerning the men who had followed Him during the days of His flesh, He reports an amazing thing: "They have kept thy word." Reflecting back upon the ways of these weak men, we think of their selfish ambitions, their frequent failure to receive the truth, their quarreling at the Last Supper, the impending denial of Peter and the doubtings of Thomas. Yet the Lord, who knows the hearts of all men, beholds these weak and vacillating men lovingly, and says, "They have kept thy word"!

Surely this judgment is not based upon any legalistic balance between so many things done and so many things left undone, but rather upon the state of the heart and the direction of the life course. They loved the Lord and treasured His words and they were faced in the right direction.

6. The will of God revealed in the written Word must always be seen in the context of God's grace. I have already touched upon this, but now we shall discuss the matter at some length. Nothing could be more crucial. Unless we see the will of God "in the context of His grace," we shall always be in

danger of reverting to old systems of legalism or building new ones. If we center upon the "will of God" and ignore that "context of grace," it is possible to erect a legalistic system even on such books as Romans and Galatians!

But consider now how carefully the Scriptures put the will of God in the context of His grace. In Romans 12:1-2 we are besought to realize the "will of God," but the exhortation comes to us "by the mercies of God." In I Corinthians 8:7-11 we are taught how careful we should be in our treatment of "weaker brethren," and the ultimate argument used is that the weak brother is one "for whom Christ died." In Philippians 2:2-5 the writer exhorts us to a life of love and forbearance, to be concerned with the good of others rather than our own things.

And how is this lofty ideal to be reached? The apostle approaches his readers through the love and mercies they have found in Christ (Phil. 2:1), and he closes the appeal by setting before their eyes the gracious condescension of the Son of God as He stoops from God to humanity, and then from humanity to death, even the death of the cross (Phil. 2:5-8).

In Philippians 4:1-3 Paul writes to bring together two women in the church who have had a falling-out. He tells them to "be of the same mind," but that is not enough. They are to be of the same mind "in the Lord," and the apostle closes by reminding them both that their "names are in the book of life." What an argument! Two women whose names by the grace of God are written in the book of life, but they have failed to be gracious to each other with their names written on one church roll! Literally hundreds of other examples may be found by the diligent reader of the New Testament writings.

In the progress of revelation there will be found, of course, certain sharp contrasts between the Age of the Law and the present age. Thus in Deuteronomy 6:5 the great obligation of man is stated in blinding severity, unrelieved by any color of grace: "Thou shalt love the LORD thy God with all thine heart, and with all thy soul, and with all thy might." Contrast the language of grace: "We love him, because he first loved us" (I John 4:19). The passage from Deuteronomy brings us into the presence of a "great white throne"; the passage from John's pen puts "a rainbow round about the throne." If we are wise, we shall always read the two texts together.

Take another example: Our Lord Jesus Christ, speaking of man's obligation to his fellowmen, lays down the second great commandment, "Thou shalt love thy neighbour as thyself" (Matt. 22:39). This is the law—the law of God. And we dare not and cannot change it. But come on this side of Calvary and hear the voice of the same Lord as He speaks through John, "Beloved, if God so loved us, we ought also to love one another" (I John 4:11). It is the same duty, but now enshrined in the context of grace. Take another example, this time from the Sermon on the Mount, "Therefore all things whatsoever ye would that men should do to you, do

ye even so to them: for this is the law and the
prophets" (Matt. 7:12). It is a good law, but there
is something higher, "Let each esteem other better
than themselves" (Phil. 2:3).

The law gives us the careful balance of justice,
but the exhortation of grace is reckless in its demand. Grace works because it is set in a "context
of grace"—the blessed Son of God laying aside His
preexistent glory, making Himself of no reputation,
taking the form of a bondservant, humbling Himself to death for us who deserve nothing (Phil. 2:3-
8). This is the argument of grace, and it is irre-
sistible for those who have been saved and know
the Lord. To it there is no answer apart from hum-
ble submission "in lowliness of mind."

But although dispensational distinctions are genuine and may be clearly observed, we are not to
suppose that the "context of grace" is completely
absent from the earlier parts of Scripture. Paul,
speaking of the Age of the Law, observes, "Moreover the law entered, that the offence might
abound." Then he adds, "But where sin abounded,
grace did much more abound" (Rom. 5:20). If you
wonder how grace abounded even in the Age of
Law, you need only read the record of the ceremonial law of sacrifice. It is here that we may find
that "context of grace" in the midst of law. Consider, for example, the giving of the Decalogue,
those "ten words" which constitute the very center
of the law. The record is found in the 20th chapter
of Exodus. Tragically, most sermons on the Ten
Commandments end with verse 17. And the result

is often the same as that found in the history of Israel. "The people . . . removed, and stood *afar off*" (v. 18). This is the result of the preaching of law apart from the context of grace.

But in verse 24 the God of Sinai speaks again, "An altar of earth thou shalt make unto me, and shalt sacrifice thereon thy burnt-offerings . . . and I will bless thee." The altar was to be made of "earth," the one material within the reach of all! But if "stone" should be used, no tool was to be used to shape it, for to do so would be to "pollute" it. Moreover, there could not be "steps" up to reach the altar. Surely, this is the language of God's grace! And what a pity that so many preachers, on the assumption that we are yet under the "moral" law but done with the "ceremonial" law, go on preaching the commandments of God without the context of grace, thus omitting the one factor which is able to secure the fullest realization of the ideal of moral law.

The truth, of course, is that the Christian is not under law in any sense, whether moral or ceremonial. But on the other hand, both elements of the law continue to be essential parts of the total written Word of God down to the last "jot and tittle," and as such it is "profitable" to all the children of God in every age.

In this connection I would like to encourage Christians who delight in finding the Lord Jesus Christ upon every page of Scripture. Do not permit yourselves to be frightened by those over-cautious souls who cry against what they call "too much typology." Doubtless there are some things which may properly be catalogued as "types" and others not. But whatever you may call it, it is the privilege and highest duty of the Christian to discover and behold the face of the Lord Jesus in Scripture—everywhere! Far better to break a few rules of classical hermeneutics than to miss the vision of His blessed face.

We need only one caution—let us be sure that what we find is always true to the historic revelation of the Son as recorded in the New Testament. With this safeguard, there is no end to what we may find in the inspired record of the infinite and incarnate Son of God. And by finding Him throughout Scripture, we shall be finding the perfect will of God in the wonderful context of His grace. For grace reigns "through righteousness unto eternal life by Jesus Christ our Lord" (Rom. 5:21) .

7. This context of grace is the only environment in which the will of God can be most fully realized in the Christian life. In this context of grace we grow (II Peter 3:18) ; we stand (I Peter 5:12) ; we are built up (Acts 20:32) ; we are made strong (II Tim. 2:1) ; we are made perfect (I Peter 5:10) ; we find freedom from sin's dominion (Rom. 6:14) ; we find complete liberty from legal bondage (Gal. 5:1-4) ; we find a sufficient motive for doing the will of God (II Cor. 8:9) ; we find an enabling power for Christian living (II Cor. 12:9) ; we find recovery when we fall (Heb. 4:16) ; we find assurance as to the final outcome of the Christian life (Acts 20:32) .

Let us take care to follow the counsel of the Apostle Paul, given to Christian believers in the midst of conflict with legalistic troublemakers, "Continue in the grace of God" (Acts 13:43). And let us be cautious of those who offer any other counsel. Paul writes with deep indignation against those who urged a departure, seemingly very small, from the gospel of the grace of God (Gal. 4:9-12).

CHAPTER 10

Objections, Questions and Problems

IN CONCLUSION, I wish to answer some common objections, questions and problems.

1. The charge has been made that in affirming the believer is not under law we are rejecting a part of Scripture. This slanderous charge has been answered already by the Biblical evidence presented earlier, but I wish to deal with it more specifically.

First, we deny categorically any rejection of the law. On the contrary, we accept the law of God in Scripture in its totality, including all its elements—moral, ceremonial and civil—not merely a small part of the law stripped of its penalties, as our opponents are accustomed to do. They, not we, are the real rejectors of the law!

Second, we accept this total divine law as a part of the inspired Word of God. Therefore it is "profitable" for all Christian believers, to be used under the guidance of the Holy Spirit for "doctrine, . . . reproof, . . . correction . . . [and] instruction in righteousness" (II Tim. 3:16). No part of the Word of God—not even the ceremonial law—can be neglected in our teaching and preaching without spiritual loss.

Third, we accept this law of God as something "good, if a man use it lawfully" (I Tim. 1:8). For the meaning of the term "lawfully" (*nomimos*) see II Timothy 2:5, where it must unquestionably carry the idea "according to law." Therefore, to use the law "according to law" must mean that it should be used *as law*, not emasculated of any of its elements or penalties.

This proper use of the law is further elaborated in I Timothy. If used lawfully, that is, strictly as law, "the law is not made for a righteous man" (I Tim. 1:9). And since the Christian believer is "righteous" in relation to the law as law (because through the work of Christ the law was completely fulfilled and satisfied for us in all its demands and penalties), it is a wrong use of the law to put the Christian *under* it. To apply the law as law to the Christian is to deny the eternal efficacy of the work of Christ. On the other hand, argues the apostle, the law as law was made "for the lawless and disobedient, for the ungodly and for sinners" (I Tim. 1:9). And he is careful to point out that in the long category of human wickedness which renders men subject to the divine law of external restraint all this is "contrary to [the] sound doctrine; according to the glorious gospel of the blessed God" (I Tim. 1:9-11).

In this same context the apostle is careful to state the simple standard of life for Christian believers: It is "charity [love] out of a pure heart, and of a good conscience, and of faith unfeigned" (I Tim. 1:5).

But even in Paul's day there were some who were not satisfied with this simple rule of life. These had "turned aside unto vain janglings; desiring to be teachers of the law [lit. *law-teachers*]; understanding neither what they say, nor whereof they affirm" (vv. 6-7) .

To summarize: In relation to the Christian, the law, *as law,* having been completely fulfilled and satisfied in Christ, has been "done away." But as law it still remains to operate as an external restraint upon the ungodly. On the other hand, the law, *as inspired Scripture,* abides for all the saved and as such is "profitable" in all its parts. Only the soul saved by grace, understanding clearly what took place at Calvary, can truly delight in the law of the Lord. Such a one has seen in the cross the awful severity and doom of the law and rejoices in the assurance that its demands have been satisfied to the last farthing by the Lamb of God.

2. It also has been said that since many professing Christians are not living as they should, the law should be used to remedy this situation. Here we must admit the problem, even while we deplore the situation. Every faithful pastor faces it, often to a degree which is almost heartbreaking. But we also know that the remedy for this shameful condition in the professing church is not to turn from grace back to the method of law. The way of law has already been demonstrated historically as utterly powerless to make men good. "The law made nothing perfect" (Heb. 7:19) . That is why the grace of God was manifested in Christ to do "what the law could not do" (Rom. 8:3) . The remedy for sin is not more law but more grace. "Where sin abounded, grace did much more abound" (Rom. 5:20) .

3. If you preach the grace of God for salvation, you will be warned that some may use the doctrine of grace as license to go on sinning. Here again we admit the warning is often based on fact. Even in the early church there were some who actually had turned "the grace of our God into lasciviousness" (Jude 4). But in the case of such men, the basic trouble was not merely that they had broken the moral law (for in this sense all have sinned), but rather that they were "denying our only Master and Lord, Jesus Christ" (Jude 4, ASV). They were "ungodly men," Jude writes, not saved men at all, "before of old ordained to this condemnation." Distressing as such cases are, it will do no good at all to change our message from grace back to law. Such a retreat can only deepen the disaster. Certainly these high-handed sinners should be warned of their final doom and urged to flee to Christ from the wrath to come. But we as preachers must never forget that the law can neither regenerate men nor make them good. Only the grace of God in Christ can do that.

4. Furthermore, if you preach this gospel of God's grace, you are likely to be charged with antinomianism. But this charge is nothing new in the history of the church. The Apostle Paul himself was accused of the same thing (Rom. 3:8). Therefore we need not be too much surprised to meet the same charge today. As a matter of fact, unless you are charged thus sooner or later you are probably not preaching the good news of God's grace as it ought to be preached. For it has been truly pointed out

that only the true doctrine of grace can be cari-
catured as a form of antinomianism. You may be
sure you will never be charged with antinomianism
as long as you are willing to compromise the message of grace with the smallest modicum of law.
But the charge is false when leveled against the
preacher of salvation by grace. For in the gospel
of salvation by grace alone in Christ we are honor-
ing the law and establishing the law. By His death
our Lord Jesus Christ satisfied in full all the law's
holy and just demands.

The real antinomians are the legalists, for they
either take only one element of the law, or they
strip it of its penalties or they soften and relax its
demands; to this extent they are *against* (Greek
"anti") the law.

5. You will also be told that, in refusing to put
Christians under law, you are lowering the standards of the good life. Actually, however, we are not
lowering the moral standards, but *raising* them.
The standard of law was "Love thy neighbor as thyself," but the rule of grace as laid down by our
Lord Jesus is "That ye love one another, as I have
loved you" (John 15:12). The difference is almost infinite. It is not the law, but Christ, dying
under the law for us and in our stead, who sets the
standard of the good life in the gospel of grace. Let
all who may have any doubts about this matter turn
again to the great passage in Philippians 2:5-11,
reading it carefully and prayerfully. Here we have
something that no mere moralist ever imagined—
not only an infinitely high rule of goodness, but also

an infinitely powerful incentive which ever lifts the sinner toward the goal of perfection.

6. But, some will say: Does not the Bible command us to fulfill the "law of Christ"? The sole basis for this idea is found in the King James Version of Galatians 6:2. The Greek verb here is almost certainly a future indicative, not an imperative. Those interested in the textual argument will find it discussed in Ellicott's Commentary on the passage. Meyer accepts the indicative reading without discussion. In the influence of early legalistic tendencies, we can account for the scribal change from the indicative to an imperative. Thus we have in Galatians 6:2 a simple statement of fact—in bearing one another's burdens, *we shall* fulfill the law of Christ.

But more important still is the question: What is this "law of Christ"? In seeking an answer it should be noted that nearly all the commentators who deal with the question at all find a reference to our Lord's words: "A new commandment I give unto you, That ye love one another; as I have loved you, that ye also love one another" (John 13:34), and "This is my commandment, That ye love one another, as I have loved you" (John 15:12). John undoubtedly refers to this same thing when he writes: "And this is his commandment, That we should believe on the name of his Son Jesus Christ, and love one another, as he gave us commandment" (I John 3:23).

Love for one's neighbor was nothing new, for it was the second great commandment of the law of Moses. What was absolutely new was this obligation of loving others as Christ has loved us. This, then, is the "law of Christ"; not the Decalogue, nor even the Sermon on the Mount, but the law of love according to a new and divine measure, namely, that we should love one another as Christ loved us.

We should also notice that the New Testament treats this law of love as the fulfillment of all other divine law dealing with human relationships. We are exhorted to "Owe no man any thing, but to love one another; for he that loveth another hath fulfilled the law. . . . Love is the fulfilling of the law" (Rom. 13:8, 10). Again the apostle exhorts us to "use not liberty for an occasion to the flesh, but by love serve one another. For all the law is fulfilled in one word, even in this; Thou shalt love thy neighbour as thyself" (Gal. 5:13-14). That this is no reversion to a former legalism is clear from the context. For this life of love is to be realized as we "walk in the Spirit" (Gal. 5:16); and "if ye be led of the Spirit, ye are not under the law" (Gal. 5:18).

Nothing could be clearer than Paul's word on the good life in his first letter to Timothy: The Christian life is to be a life of "love"; and this love rises in its ultimate source out of "unfeigned faith." It is not something worked up in any mechanical fashion. Furthermore, the apostle writes, this "love" is actually "the end of the commandment." It comprehends everything of value in the realm of Christian ethics, and beyond it there is nothing.

We close the discussion of this point by calling attention to a rather curious and striking thing:

While we are commanded to love one another, and this love is the fulfillment of the law, nowhere are we commanded to "fulfill the law"! The proper Christian formula is set forth in Romans 8:1-4, ASV:

a. We are told that there can be no condemnation to them which are in Christ Jesus.

b. The reason for this exemption is found in our freedom from the law, which in fallen man could only stimulate sin and finally bring death.

c. What that law could not do, God in Christ did for us at Calvary, when He was made an offering for sin.

d. The moral result of this way of saving men is that the righteousness of the law is "fulfilled in us." The verb is passive, not active in form. "It is not our doing, though done in us.[20]

7. Perhaps the commonest objection to the doctrine of salvation by grace without the law is that such preaching may turn out to be morally dangerous. People may argue, as some did in the days of Paul, that since the grace of God is always greater than all our sin, why not go on sinning that grace may abound? Is there not therefore a danger that men may say: "Let us do evil, that good may come" (Rom. 3:8) ?

In replying to this objection we may say, first, that the doctrine of salvation by grace without the law may indeed be dangerous for some people. For that matter, all divine truth is dangerous to those

[20]Denny, "Romans," *The Expositor's Greek Testament,* II, 646, v. 4.

who resist or reject or misuse it. The same gospel which is a savor of life to those who believe is also a savor of death to all who reject it (II Cor. 3:15-16). Surely it is folly to suggest that we should cease to teach divine truth because there are some who pervert it. The Apostle Paul had to deal with such people in his day, and his ultimatum was brief and to the point—"whose damnation is just," he writes (Rom. 3:8). It is a waste of time and breath to argue with people who will stoop to pervert the truth in the interest of immorality.

But on the other hand, for the true Christian this doctrine of salvation by grace without the law is not dangerous. But anything else is dangerous, for the simple reason that only the grace of God in Christ can break the power of sin and transform our lives into the image of His Son. Reversion to methods of law can only compound the moral disaster, for "the strength of sin is the law" (I Cor. 15:56). Not that the law of God is evil. His law is holy and good. But *we* are evil, so terribly evil that even the holy prohibitions of divine law can only arouse the worst that is in us—"When the commandment came, sin revived. . . . And the commandment, which was ordained to life, I found to be unto death" (Rom. 7:9-10). Not the law, but only grace, can give us moral victory. "For sin shall not have dominion over you: for ye are not under the law, but under grace" (Rom. 6:14).

It is utterly false to argue, as some do, that the doctrine of salvation by grace alone will lead Christian people to go on sinning. Grace does not teach

God's people to sin. Grace teaches them *not* to sin. "For the grace of God that bringeth salvation hath appeared to all men, teaching us [who believe] that, denying ungodliness and worldly lusts, we should live soberly, righteously, and godly, in this present world; looking for that blessed hope, and the glorious appearing of the great God and our Saviour Jesus Christ" (Tit. 2:11-13) .

8. Doesn't I Corinthians 9:20-21 say that Christians are under the law? Those who are legalistically inclined have leaned heavily upon this passage for support. It reads as follows in the King James Version (vv. 20-21) : "And unto the Jews I became as a Jew, that I might gain the Jews; to them that are under the law, as under the law, that I might gain them that are under the law; To them that are without law, as without law, (being not without law to God, but under the law to Christ,) that I might gain them that are without law."

This is the only text in the King James Version that seems to say that Christians are "under the law." Although the Greek is confessedly difficult, I feel that the translators could have at least indicated to the English reader that the Greek expression translated "under the law to Christ" is totally different from the ordinary formula. "Under the law" in verse 21 represents but one Greek word, *"ennomos,"* whereas the ordinary formula is *"upo nomos."* See verse 20, where it occurs three times and is properly rendered each time "under the law."

What did Paul mean when he wrote "being not without law to God, but under the law to Christ" in verse 21? It is a matter of interest here that not only "under the law" but also "without law" represents only one Greek word—"under the law" is *"ennomos,"* while "without law" is *"anomos."*

It is also generally agreed among the editors of the Greek text that the words "God" and "Christ" here are in the genitive rather than the dative case. Thus the passage might be literally translated, "Not being an out-law of God, but an in-law of Christ."[21] It is not *where* we are, but *what* we are in relation to Christ.

Whatever the passage means, it cannot mean that Paul was asserting that he was *"upo nomos"*—"under the law." For, as I have pointed out above, not only does Paul *not* say this in the original, but in verse 20 he declares that he himself is "not . . . under the law"! See the verse in the American Standard Version. Although the clause does not appear in the King James Version, all the Greek editors agree that the manuscript evidence is overwhelming in its support. Therefore the revisers included it without any indication whatever that there was any question.

Why was the clause omitted from some manuscripts? The omission points rather strongly to a tampering with the text on the part of some legalistically inclined copyist. But the Word of God is living and cannot be bound. It arises to confound all those who would suppress or destroy it.

[21]See A. T. Robertson, *Word Pictures in the New Testament* (New York: Harper & Bros., 1931), IV, 147, v. 21.